To

Meagan

From

Granma & Granpa Donnelly

Date 12 - 25 -93

Praise

The Helen Steiner Rice Foundation

Whatever the celebration, whatever the day, whatever the event, whatever the occasion, Helen Steiner Rice possessed the ability to express the appropriate feeling for that particular moment in time.

A happening became happier, a sentiment more sentimental, a memory more memorable because of her deep sensitivity to put into understandable language the emotion being experienced. Her positive attitude, her concern for others, and her love of God are identifiable threads woven into her life, her works . . . and even her death.

Prior to her passing, she established the HELEN STEINER RICE FOUNDATION, a nonprofit corporation whose purpose is to award grants to worthy charitable programs and aid the elderly, the needy, and the poor. In her lifetime, these were the individuals about whom Mrs. Rice was greatly concerned.

Royalties from the sale of this book will add to the financial capabilities of the HELEN STEINER RICE FOUNDATION. Each year this foundation presents grants to various qualified, worthwhile, and charitable programs. Because of her foresight, her caring, and her deep convictions, Helen Steiner Rice continues to touch a countless number of lives. Thank you for your assistance in helping to keep Helen's dream alive.

Virginia J. Ruehlmann, Administrator
The Helen Steiner Rice Foundation
Suite 2100, Atrium Two
221 East Fourth Street
Cincinnati, Ohio 45202

Precious Moments of Praise

Verses *by* Helen Steiner Rice

Compiled *by* Virginia J. Ruehlmann

Illustrations *by* Samuel J. Butcher

Fleming H. Revell
A Division of Baker Book House
Grand Rapids, Michigan 49516

The endsheets,
enhanced with real flower petals,
ferns, and other botanicals,
are from
"The Petals Everlasting Collection"
manufactured by Permalin Products.

Text copyright 1993 by Helen Steiner Rice Foundation
Art copyright 1993 by PRECIOUS MOMENTS, Inc.

Published by Fleming H. Revell,
a division of Baker Book House
P.O. Box 6287, Grand Rapids, Michigan 49516-6287

Library of Congress Cataloging-in-Publication Data

Rice, Helen Steiner.
    Precious moments of praise / verses by Helen Steiner Rice ; compiled by Virginia J.
Ruehlmann ; illustrations by Samuel J. Butcher.
        p.   cm.
    ISBN 0-8007-1693-0
    1. Christian poetry, American. I. Ruehlmann, Virginia J. II. Butcher, Samuel J.
(Samuel John), 1939–   . III. Title.
PS3568.I28P748   1993
811'.54—dc20   93-12070

Printed in the United States of America

Contents

Be glad   9

In the beauty of a snowflake   12

I come not to ask   14

Springtime is a season   16

Dear God, there are things we cannot measure   20

The good green earth beneath our feet   22

Apple blossoms bursting wide   24

Thank You, God   26

Where there is love   30

Good morning, God   40

God's love   42

"The earth is the Lord's"   52

"Jesus loves me"   58

Nature's greatest forces   62

I see the dew glisten   64

$\mathcal{B}$e
glad
that you've had such a full, happy life.
Be glad
for your joy as well as your strife.
Be glad
that you've walked in sunshine and rain.
Be glad
that you've felt both pleasure and pain.

9

Be glad
that you've tasted the bitter and sweet.
Be glad
that your life has been full and complete.
Be glad
that you've walked with courage each day.
Be glad
you've had strength for each step of the way.

Be glad
for the comfort you've found in prayer.
But be happiest
of all for
God's tender care.

In the beauty of a snowflake
falling softly on the land
is the mystery
and the miracle
of God's great, creative hand.

In the tiny petal
of a tiny flower
that grew from a tiny pod
is the
miracle
and the
mystery
of
all creation
and
God.

I come not to ask,
to plead,
or implore You.
I just come to tell you
how much
I adore You.
For to kneel in Your presence
makes me feel blest,
and I know that You know
all my needs best.
And it fills me with joy
just to linger with You
as my soul You replenish
and my heart You renew.

For prayer is much more than
just asking for things.
It's the peace
and contentment
that quietness brings.
So thank You again
for your mercy and love.
And for making me heir
to Your kingdom above.

Springtime is a season
of hope
and joy
and cheer.
There's beauty all around us
to see and touch and hear.

So, no matter how
downhearted and discouraged
we may be,
new hope is born
when we behold
leaves budding on a tree.

Or when we see a timid flower
push through the frozen sod
and open wide in glad surprise
its petaled eyes to God.

For this is just God saying,
"Lift up your eyes to me.
And the bleakness of your spirit,
like the budding springtime tree,
will lose its wintry darkness
and your heavy heart will sing."
For God never sends the winter
without the joy of spring.

$\mathcal{D}$ear God,
there are things we cannot measure,
like the depths and waves of sea
and the heights of stars in heaven
and the joy You bring to me.

Like eternity's long endlessness
and the sunset's golden hue,
there is no better way to measure
the love I have for You.

The good green earth beneath our feet,
the air we breathe,
the food we eat,
some work to do,
a goal to win,
a hidden longing deep within
that spurs us on to bigger things

and helps us meet
what each day brings,
all these things
and many more
are things we should be thankful for.
And most of all our thankful prayers
arise to God
because
He
cares.

Apple blossoms bursting wide
now beautify the tree
and make a springtime picture
that is beautiful to see.

Oh, fragrant, lovely blossoms,
you'll make a bright bouquet
if I but break your branches
from the apple tree today.
But if I break your branches
and make your beauty mine,
you'll bear no fruit in season
when severed from the vine.

Thank You, God,
for little things
that often come our way.

The things we take for granted
but don't mention
when we pray.

The unexpected courtesy,
the thoughtful, kindly deed,
a hand reached out to help us
in the time of sudden need.

Oh, make us more aware,
dear God,
of little daily graces
that come to us
with sweet surprise
from never-dreamed-of places.

Where there is love
the heart is light.

31

Where there is love
the day is bright.

Where there is love
there is a song
to help when things
are
going
wrong.

Where there is love
there is a smile
to make all things
seem more worthwhile.

Where there is love
there's quiet peace,
a tranquil place
where turmoils cease.

Love changes darkness into light
and makes the heart take
wingless flight.
Oh, blest are they who walk in love.
They also walk with God above.
And when man walks with God again,
There shall be peace on earth
for men.

$\mathcal{G}$ood morning, God!
You are
ushering in a new day
untouched
and freshly new.
So here I come
to ask You, God,
if
You'll renew me, too.
Forgive the many errors
that I made yesterday.
And let me try again, dear God,
to walk closer in Your way.

But, Father,
I am well aware
I can't make it on my own.
So take my hand
and
hold it tight
for I can't walk alone.

God's love
is like an island
in life's ocean vast and wide—
a peaceful, quiet shelter
from the restless, rising tide.

God's love
is like an anchor
when the angry billows roll—
a mooring in the storms of life,
a stronghold for the soul.

God's love
is like a fortress
and we seek protection there
when the waves of tribulation
seem to drown us in despair.

God's love
is like a harbor
where our souls can find sweet rest
from the struggle and the tension
of life's fast and futile quest.

God's love
is like a beacon
burning bright with faith and prayer
and through the changing scenes of life
we can find a haven there.

"The earth is the Lord's
and the fulness thereof."
It speaks of His greatness
and sings of His love.

54

And the wonder and glory
of the first Easter morn,
like the first Christmas night
when the Savior was born,
are blended together
in symphonic splendor.
And God with a voice
that is gentle and tender
speaks to all hearts
attuned to His voice,
bidding His listeners
to gladly rejoice.

For He who was born
to be crucified
Arose from the grave
to be glorified.
And the birds in the trees
and the flowers of spring
all join in proclaiming
this heavenly king.

"Jesus loves me, this I know,
for the Bible tells me so."
Little children ask no more,
for
love is
all they're looking for.

And in a small child's shining eyes
the faith of all the ages lies.
And tiny hands and tousled heads
that
kneel in prayer
by little beds
are closer to the dear Lord's heart
and of His kingdom more a part
than we who search and never find
the answers
to
our questioning mind.

For faith in things we cannot see
requires a child's simplicity.
And with a small child's trusting eyes,
may all men come to realize
that faith alone can save a soul
and lead us
to
a higher goal.

Nature's greatest forces
are found in quiet things
like
softly
falling
snowflakes
drifting down on
angels' wings.

Or petals
dropping soundlessly
from a lovely
full-blown rose.
So God comes closest to us
when our souls are in repose.

I see the dew glisten
as a new day is born.
And I hear the birds sing
on the wings of the morn
as God wraps up the night
and tucks it away
and hands out the sun
to herald a new day.
A day yet unblemished
by what's gone before.
A chance to begin
and start over once more.
And all I need do
is to silently pray,
"God, help me and guide me
and go with me today."